T0392304

AuthorHouse™ UK
1663 Liberty Drive
Bloomington, IN 47403 USA
www.authorhouse.co.uk
Phone: 0800.197.4150

Scripture quotations marked KJV are from the Holy Bible, King James Version (Authorized Version). First published in 1611. Quoted from the KJV Classic Reference Bible, Copyright © 1983 by The Zondervan Corporation.

Illustrations done by
Name Bede-Nwokoye, Ogochukwu
Email: ogobedenwokoye@gmail.com
Mobile: +2348033201167

Published by AuthorHouse 06/27/2019

ISBN: 978-1-7283-8852-6 (sc)
ISBN: 978-1-7283-8851-9 (e)

This book has been catalogued with the United States Library of Congress
Library of Congress Control Number: 2019905943

Print information available on the last page.

Any people depicted in stock imagery provided by Getty Images are models,
and such images are being used for illustrative purposes only.
Certain stock imagery © Getty Images.

This book is printed on acid-free paper.

The author obtained the information contained there in from the sources she believes are reliable and from her own personal experience working with teenagers in two decades. The author also disclaims any liabilities caused by the information contained herein.

authorHOUSE®

THE COMPASS:

For Teenagers and Young Adults

Crossing the Bridge to Adulthood

UDUAK ESSEN

Credit for all drawings:

Bede-Nwokoye, Ogochukwu

Twitter @BedeNwokoye

All Bible quotations are from the King James Version

This book is dedicated to all teenagers and young adults—my friends!

I also dedicate this book to my late daughter, Hallel; your memory lives on.

Table of Contents

Acknowledgement

I thank the Almighty God for the unction and grace to document my interactions with teenagers and young adults spanning about two decades in this book.

I also appreciate my spiritual fathers who have spoken into my life and encouraged me in one way or the other through their teachings and books which have formed a rock-solid foundation for daily living and springboard for mentoring. They include Bishop David and Faith Oyedepo, Bishop David and Pastor (Mrs) Mary Abioye , Bishop and Pastor (Mrs) Thomas Aremu, Pastor Abraham Ojeme, Pastor and Dcns Moses Oyedele, Pastor and Dcns John Adelekan, Pastor and Dcns Olushola Adeleye, Pastor and Dcns Chris Iyeke, Pastor and Dcns Raymond Ekunode all of Living Faith Church, Pastor (Dr) & Dr (Mrs) Paul & Becky Enenche of Dunamis International Gospel Ministry, Pastor and Mrs David Ibiyeome of Salvation Ministries, and Pastor and Mrs Udeme Wisdom Anaka of Flame of God's Glory International Ministry your prayers have brought me here. Thank you, Pastor and Mrs James John of Awesome Chapel, for believing that God has deposited something in me for teenagers and young adults which the world needs to read about.

To my father Bishop David Abioye, for the loaded and tremendous foreword you carefully penned for the contemporary teenager, your teachings that have been a recipe for mentoring teenagers and young adults over the years, your prophetic declarations and prayers that have hastened the manifestation of *the compass*, may God bless you beyond measure.

A huge appreciation goes to my mentors, Barr Isaac and Jan Okpanachi, and late Reverend Chris Agape Ajah, who showed me the way of the Lord during my teenage years; your labour was not in vain.

My gratitude goes to my parents, my late father Mr Bassey Etuk and my mother Mrs Eno Bassey, for a job well done in showing me the way of the Lord early with a recipe to ensure I stood firm in the Lord as a child, a teenager and now an adult. To my children Emmanuella, Favour and Davida, I love you all and acknowledge your contributions and consistent encouragements to me to ensure other teenagers and young adults like you read this book and learn as well.

Ogochukwu Bede-Nwokoye, an architect and illustrator, thank you for the pictorial display of the chapters.

To my indefatigable and inspiring friends, Dr Ekanem Onyemaechi, Dr Nse Onyebuchi, Arc (Mrs) Veronica Eke, Arc (Mrs) Ngodoo Ayilla, Mrs Ngozichukwu Etuk , Perptua Amodu and Amos Jackson for consistently inspiring and praying that this book becomes a reality, to bless teenagers, God bless you!

Thank you Dr Akudo Ikpeazu for your gift of thoroughness and confidence that rubbed off on me and emboldened the birthing of *The Compass*. Pastor Francis Agbo and Madam Jane Ezenekwe, thank you for strongly encouraging me and now *The Compass* has been transformed from a manuscript to a published book.

Thanks to everyone at Author House UK that was part of the process and the rigor of publishing; you all treated me and my work with great dignity, deep respect and integrity.

To all who contributed in different ways but not mentioned here, God bless you all.

Finally, to my husband Dr Nyomudim who has been a spiritual pillar, a physical anchor, and early support with strong resolve that set *The Compass* ball rolling, thank you for who you are and all you do.

Foreword

From biblical and natural points of view, life is a journey with a beginning and definite end. It is a race filled with diverse experiences, opportunities as well as challenges, all of which summed up to define who we are as humans, how we live and who we eventually become.

By virtue of certain peculiarities, life is categorised into phases or stages, and the scriptures in **1 John 2:13-14**, also emphasized the significance of each stage, *"I write unto you, <u>fathers</u>, because ye have known him that is from the beginning. I write unto you, <u>young men (teenagers)</u>, because ye have overcome the wicked one. I write unto you, little <u>children</u>, because ye have known the Father. I write unto you, father, because ye have known him that is from the beginning. I have written unto you, young men, because ye are strong..." (emphasis mine)*

The teenager is the inception of youthful stage which is very essential and symbolic; it is the bridge between babyhood and childhood where we are under tutors and care-givers and adulthood, where we graduate into independence and being looked up to by others for guidance, direction and support.

It is therefore imperative for teenagers to begin to see life with an eye of future, responsibility, discipline and determination. If this 'bridge' is shaky, disjointed and broken, it means the next phase of life (adulthood) will be impaired hence the kind of adults we see in our society today. How important is it for youths to realize that life is lived only once, with no option for a second chance?

The teenage years are adventurous years where youths try to experiment with many things to determine their preferences, no doubt about that. But, teenage years are never meant to be playful or indiscipline years, if one would grow up to become responsible and respectable adult. This is why all youths especially teenagers must mind how they culture themselves at this crucial stage of their lives. Whatever one becomes as an adult is a function of choices made at this moment of life.

Of course, there is no generation that has ever been free from evil tendencies since creation: time of Cain and Abel, Joseph, David, Daniel, etc. Evil is not new but falling for it or standing against it is simply a matter of choice. No excuse is tenable for allowing negative influences to infringe on your dignity as a teenager. Pressure from society or peers should never be allowed to push any teenage into temptations, so as to become significant by the world standard.

All of these and so much more, is what the author of this book, **The Compass**, has succeeded in shedding more light on them, in order to awaken in our teenagers, need to be rightly motivated into following the good paths of life, towards becoming responsible adults in future.

As you go through it, may you find meaning and be motivated to building lasting virtues and values of life that will engender positive results in your regret-free adulthood.

David O. Abioye

Abuja, Nigeria.

May, 2019

Introduction

Life is a journey. Life is precious and sweet. No matter how you have lived, it is important to remember you will have to account for it someday.

Your life has a beginning and an end. The period from the beginning to the end requires a careful walk with the Maker to ensure you reach your destination without missing the mark. How you have lived your life so far is a good predictor of how it could possibly end.

Being a teenager is exciting, but it also has its challenges and pressure points, with so many things happening almost at the same time. The teenage phase is characterized by a surge in sex hormone levels, the subsequent development of the secondary sexual characteristics, and the appearance of adult features. These attendant changes both physically and emotionally give the teenager the feeling of *I am now an adult* or *I am now grown up.*

Teenagers are not only special but also daring and ready to take risks, so this period comes with peer pressure and vices; you will require the help and godly tutelage of your parents or guardian to properly guide you through this phase. These adults each passed through these challenges to be where and who they are today, so they can provide proper guidance to teens as they cross the teenage bridge with its associated inner struggles and turbulence.

Someone once said, "We are children for a very short time, teenagers for a while, and when we become adults, we stay as adults for so many years." It is important to note that what you do in your teenage years will seriously shape your adult years. Are you laying the right foundation? Are you navigating your life path with the right compass? Are you doing it yourself as a *do-it-yourself* (DIY) person? When I was a teen, my generation had hardly any literature to read for guidance. We navigated the teenage era like people groping in the dark with passed-down dos and don'ts from Mum!

Human beings are made up of a spirit with a soul and live in a body. God is interested in your relationship with Him because He desires to guide you and other humans through the vagaries of life. He is interested in where your soul ends up after life's sojourn, as well as what emotions, pains, and plans you have. He has a deep interest in you because He cares about you.

This book is in no way exhaustive, but it does provide navigation paths for teens and young adults who live in a sexually livened world that has more questions than answers for all the teens who are bugged by enquiries. This book includes fifteen navigation paths. Each chapter is a path that readers may pass through during their teenage years. The issues this book discusses are those I have recurrently dwelt on with teenagers at different times over the years. I had a strong unction to document these experiences and interactions in a book so that I can provide a handy compass to bless teenagers and young adults wherever they are found.

I earnestly pray that you choose to navigate with God so you have a hitch-free ride in life.

Take your life very seriously. As Bishop David Abioye says, "If you take life casually, you may end up a casualty." God bless you as you navigate it.

Chapter 1: Hearing God

Hearing God is crucial because He has the blueprint of all our lives. He is our Maker (He made us; Genesis 1:38) and our Former (He formed us; Jeremiah 1:5), and He is the Potter, and all of us are the clay (Isaiah 64:8; Job 33:6). So it is important that we know what He made us to be and do, for we shall all account for our lives here on earth.

Bishop David Oyedepo has emphatically illustrated that to fully understand the workings and details of any gadget or equipment we buy, we need to go through the manual. Applying that to our lives, we can all come to understand that our manual is the Bible, which contains what He designed and wonderfully made us to do or become. Thoroughly going through that manual is key to fulfilling our destiny and reaching each of our purposes in grand style.

Hearing God involves closely walking with Him. You can work for Him and not walk with Him. Working for God is an activity, and walking with God is a relationship. Many work for God but do not walk with Him. You cannot walk with God and not work for Him! Moses, David, Daniel, Peter, Paul, Esther, and more could not have achieved the feats they did without taking a close walk with God.

> Christianity is a personal relationship with God that has become a lifestyle.
>
> —Pastor Abraham Ojeme

Is Hearing God Necessary?

Absolutely yes! It saves you a lot of mistakes, guesswork, and unnecessary heartaches in all areas of your life. Life is full of important decisions and seasons. Don't leave life's important decisions to guesswork. As the famous lyrics by Bongos Ikwue put it, "What's gonna be gonna be. What goes up must come down. … There's nothing you can do about it!" This is synonymous with not taking action and leaving everything to chance. In the words of Bishop David Abioye, "If you take life casually, you may end up a casualty."

You have something you can do in your life and about your life so you feature in a glorious destiny. Living without hearing God is like being in a car with failed brakes; you'll head for an imminent crash. Hearing God is key to achieving your glorious destiny.

How Do You Hear God?

I have often heard young people, in their innocence, exclaim, "So that very *big* God can speak to little me?" God speaks to all His children in different ways. Are you His child? You become His child when you are born again. "To as many as receive Him gave He power to become the sons of God, even to those that believe in His name" (John 1:12).

When you receive and believe God, you become His child. God speaks to His children. God speaks in many ways, and you can pick up on the signals if you are tuned to His frequency. He can speak to you anywhere. You may be in a very noisy place, for instance, but if your spirit stays quiet amid the noise, you can hear God. God spoke to John at the island of Patmos and to Moses at the burning bush, the Red Sea, and other places. It takes staying connected to God to hear Him.

How Does God Speak?

God speaks through the following means.

The Word

It is very important that you become well versed in the Word of God, so when the devil tries to alter it, you can detect it because you know the original version. A good example is found with Eve in the garden of Eden. God gave clear instructions about the fruits from which to eat and not eat (Genesis 2:16–17). However, when the serpent came to tempt Eve, he twisted the original version of God's Word to suit his deceitful schemes, and Eve fell for it (Genesis 3:3–6). When you know your Bible and live what the Bible says, you will not derail.

In whatever way God speaks to you, use the acid test to prove it is with the Bible. "God's Word is light, and its entrance giveth the same" (Psalm 119:130). God's Word is a lamp unto your feet and a light unto your path (Psalm 119:105). It is important to know that the written Word is known as *logos*, while *rhema* is a specific word of God to you for a specific purpose, not to the public. God speaks through His Word.

Dreams, Visions, and Trances

God also speaks through dreams and visions in lots of biblical examples. Note that not all dreams are God-given. A good example is Joseph's experience in the Bible. God related with him through dreams, and all his dreams came to pass. Daniel also was relevant in every government of his time because God spoke to him through dreams and visions. Joseph (husband to Mary, the mother of Jesus) got express instructions on what to do, how to do it, and where to go via dreams.

I have been privileged to have God lead me through dreams as well. In choosing a course of study at university in the 1990s, I really needed to stay on point so I didn't end up in misery, studying what God never ordained for me. I really had a strong passion for medicine and surgery, but I was not sure whether God intended that for me. I wanted to study medicine not because I was good in the sciences, but because I earnestly wanted to fulfil a purpose. As a teenager, I sincerely sought the Lord's face the way I knew how: through prayer. Everywhere I found myself and every time I remembered to do so, apart from in my formal morning prayers, I told God exactly what I wanted. I never heard anything, but I trusted God would answer even though I did not know the way the answer would come.

Then one fateful day, after I had said my nightly prayers and slept, I dreamed and saw myself amid medical doctors, all wearing clinical coats and preparing to make their rounds. Nigeria's then minister for health, who was a famous paediatrician, led us. When I woke up, it was clear to me that God had been in the dream. I got that admission without stress. And ever since, God's been faithful.

A trance is an open vision. God speaks to many people in the Bible through trances too.

Voices

Samuel audibly heard God's voice, and he fulfilled his destiny. But I am also aware that the devil deceives many with voices. You may hear yourself and then claim to have heard God. In 2017, in south-east Nigeria, an incident occurred where an older sibling claimed to have heard God instruct him to marry his sister, who was seven years younger than him. This abominable act could not have come from God, as seen in Leviticus 18:6–20. So test every spirit with the Word of God.

I am privileged to have had this experience. A remarkable incident occurred when I was on holiday during my university days. I received my medical education in south-east Nigeria, but my family resided in north-west Nigeria, which is a distance of about eight hundred kilometres. At that time, the popular means of transportation between these regions was by luxury bus. The day my holiday started, I left school for the bus station. On arrival at the bus station, I soon realised petrol was scarce, which resulted in a crowd of people who had been stranded.

After waiting for quite a long time, I saw a bus heading to north-west Nigeria arrive. As soon as I saw the bus, I was excited and heaved a sigh of relief. I silently prayed for God to grant me a favourable journey home for the holiday. No sooner had I embarked than I heard a voice saying, "Pray! Pray! Pray!" I turned to see who was talking, but everyone was minding his or her own business, and no one was looking in my direction. I soon realised it was God speaking because He had spoken to me in that fashion before. I told God I had already prayed while I was waiting for the bus to arrive. I heard it again: "Pray!" I started praying in the Spirit, this time without applying reasoning. By this time, the bus had left the station and gained good speed. I kept praying.

I had not prayed for up to forty minutes when I heard a loud noise and I saw the rims of the bus's rear tyres completely detach and roll into the oncoming lane. The driver struggled to gain control of our unbalanced bus while trying to avoid swerving into the oncoming lane. By now, almost everyone in the bus was shouting and pleading, "The blood of Jesus, the blood of Jesus," irrespective of race, religion, or anything else.

The bus finally came to a halt without somersaulting, and it was evident that the hand and presence of God in the bus averted the calamity. I was sober and then understood why God had prompted me and strongly impressed it upon me to pray. Friends, there is no substitute to hearing God!

To enjoy having God lead us whichever way He chooses, prompt obedience is paramount. Captain Ricosetta Mafella, an Indonesian pilot who usually hums worship songs during his flights, exemplifies how to promptly obey after hearing God. On the fateful day that a tsunami struck Indonesia, he audibly worshipped God. As he worshipped, he heard God say, "Get out of this place, and depart early." In prompt obedience to this divine instruction, he took off three minutes earlier than the departure time, which eventually saved the lives of the pilot and the 148 passengers on board. In Mafella's words, "God reveals everything.

If you are late for one or two seconds, it could be disaster. I don't need to prove that God is alive." Receive the grace for prompt obedience!

Circumstances

God can pass on a message through circumstances and events, such as the following:

- **Strong impressions, unctions, and an inner witness:** I hear this a lot from my teenage friends: "Something was telling me ABC would happen, and exactly that happened." That "something" is a personality—the Holy Spirit. The Holy Spirit may give you prompts and strong impressions or even an inner witness. Learn to pick up on the prompts and unctions of the Holy Ghost because He shows us things to come (John 16:13). I lived in northern Nigeria when I wedded. One year four months into the marriage, a riot occurred in our city. However, since my husband and I lived in a government reserved area setting, we considered it super safe. But God kept prompting us to remove our certificates from our residence. One Sunday after church during the riot period, I kept having strong prompts to take our certificates to a secure place. We did take the certificates out of the house that Sunday and decided to visit a family friend to see whether calm had been restored to the city. We had not spent quite an hour in the family friend's house when another friend of ours ran down, panting to inform us that hoodlums had set our residence ablaze. If we had rationalised why we should take our certificates from a super safe place, our story would have been different today.

- **Prayer and fasting:** Prayer and fasting enhance one's ability to hear God's voice (John 10:3–5, 27). You will hear God if you are His child. Fasting with prayer and with Bible study makes God send revelations your way, and it also heightens your sensitivity to divine signals. The Word of God is light, and when light enters you, every darkness disappears.

- **Fleece:** Be very careful when claiming to hear God this way. Always confirm with the Word of God that you are not hearing yourself or setting things that would favour you, which may not necessarily come from God. I know a few people who used fleece and got messed up. A certain sister who loves the Lord, having reached thirty-eight years of age and being very desperate to marry, used fleece to say, "Lord, let any man who knocks on my door early Friday morning, after my morning devotion, be the man you have sent to become my husband." Early Friday morning, a few minutes after her morning devotion, her doorbell rang. Not even knowing who was at the door, she immediately uttered, "Aha, at last my husband has finally landed." On opening the door, alas, she saw a young girl, a next-door neighbour who asked to microwave her meal for school at the woman's house since her family had just run out of gas.

Whichever medium God uses to speak to you, authenticate it with the Word of God, the Bible.

Hindrances to hearing God include the following:

- Living in sin (Sin sets a barrier between you and God. When you are separated from God, you cannot hear Him.)

- Compromising

- Disobeying

- Lacking the ability to recognise God's voice

- Not fasting with prayers

- Not studying the Word

Enablers to hearing God include the following:

- Praying and fasting

- Reading His Word

- Praising and worshipping Him

The benefits of divine direction include the following:

- It provides divine protection.

- It averts destruction.

- It averts loss.

- It prolongs our lives.

- It leads to prompt destiny fulfilment.

- It gives us the privilege of knowing the blueprint of our lives at every point in time, which can help us avoid mistakes and wrong decisions.

Action Points

- Walk with God; be His friend. Abraham walked with God, and God had this to say: "Shall I hide from Abraham that thing which I do?" (Genesis 18:17–18). Other such scriptures include Isaiah 41:8 and James 2:23.

- Learn to also discern the devil's voice because it is subtle. Weigh what you hear with God's Word.

- Read about hearing God from sound Christian authors, such as Joyce Meyer, Kenneth Hagin, David Oyedepo, Paul Enenche, and Benny Hinn.

  God speaks so learn to hear His voice. If you are not hearing Him, check to be sure you're not just practising religion.

  —Anonymous

Chapter 2: Talking to God

Prayer involves talking to God. Prayer is not a monologue but a dialogue between you and your Creator. God hears! God speaks!

You can talk to God anywhere, and you do not need to rehearse the styles in order to perfectly talk to Him. Start out in any respectful way, and be consistent.

Why Should You Pray?

Jesus Christ, who is our example, prayed while on earth and even taught us the famous Lord's Prayer. There are lots of mysteries you may not understand, but prayer resolves these mysteries. Prayer also helps you develop your spiritual muscle, which is very important in a generation such as this. Constantly communing with God would establish His fear in your heart and increase your reverence for Him, which would keep you centred on Him. That reverence for God keeps you away from evil even when you are a thousand kilometres away from home or parental care. This is having genuine fear of God, not playing church.

When you pray to God, you are, of course, talking to God, but also, when you read His Word, God is talking to you. The Word would be a lamp unto your feet and a light unto your path (Psalm 119:105).

Prayer further deepens your dependence on God and solidifies your confidence in Him.

Have You Prayed Today?

Praying daily builds your relationship with God. When you are in crisis, God will stand with and by you because you give Him His place in your life as the first choice, not the last option. Keep nurturing your relationship with God by reading His Word and spending time in His presence through prayer.

Prayer averts danger! Prayer moves mountains!

> Prayer keeps you in touch with divinity.
>
> —Uduak Essen

Action Points

- Keep a prayer log. Write down all prayer points, and when God answers them, tick them off. Thank God for the answers as well.

- Also keep a book of testimonies to document testimonies and *everything* God has done, recording the dates on which they all happen. This way, you can thank Him with understanding and not take any of His acts for granted.

- Be thankful always.

- Add fasting to your prayers; fasting suppresses the flesh and sharpens your sensitivity to catch what God says.

- Pray always, pray for everything, and pray without ceasing.

Resources

- *Power of a Praying Teen* by Stormie Omartian

Chapter 3: Goal Setting

A *goal*, by simple definition, is what you plan to achieve, but the British English Dictionary meaning of a plan is a detailed proposal for doing or achieving something. This also means that for a plan to be achievable, you need a good strategy. Whatever goals you have in life, you need a strategic plan to achieve them. You can conceive a good plan only when you start it and go through it with God.

Why You Should Set Goals

"Where there is no vision, the people perish; but he who keeps the law blessed is he" (Proverbs 29:18). It is clear that without a vision, which is synonymous with goals, people perish. In order to not perish, we need goals; with goals, we can make a meaningful impact and fulfil our destiny in grand style.

Goal setting does the following:

- It enables you to maintain focus.

- It channels your energy towards a target.

- It makes you diligent to reach the set goal.

- It motivates your persistence to achieve.

- It allows you to measure progress.

Types of goals include the following:

- **Short-term goals:** These take days, weeks, months, or one to three years to achieve.

- **Medium or intermediate goals:** These take three to five years to achieve.

- **Long-term goals:** These take five years and above to achieve.

TO DO

- GET HAIRCUT & DO MY MANICURE ☑
- ⊙ RESEARCH INTERNET ON GMAT, IELTS ☑
- GYM ☑
- MUSIC LESSONS ☐
- ⊙ BUILD GRADE POINT ☐
- ⊙ CHOOSE COURSE TO STUDY
- PRIVATE LESSONS FOR NECO WAEC, UTME
- ⊙ QUIET TIME ☑
- ⊙ SEE MENTOR

How You Set Goals

It is easy to write down your goals and assign timelines to them. If you plan to become a pilot and you are presently in junior secondary school, it will take you well over five years to achieve such a plan. Such a plan would fall into the long-term plan category.

You will necessarily need a notebook or a planner, or a digital device such as a portable document planner, to write down *all* ideas that come to you and what you really have a passion for. Seek the face of God to ask Him, the Maker of all, what exactly He made or wired you for.

It is very important that you know what you want and where you are going; if not, "everywhere and everything would look like " what you want and where you want to go (David Oyedepo). On the other hand, setting goals can also be described as having and seeing the picture of your future from scripture. Bishop David Oyedepo succinctly puts it this way: "You cannot feature in the future you have not pictured." Have a picture in mind of who and what you want to become, and run with it. You cannot miss it walking with God's blueprint.

Ayomide, a young friend of mine in her third year in junior secondary school, has dreamed of becoming a medical doctor, but she obviously has no idea what it would entail. She is quite serious about her studies but needs guidance. I told her she needs to set long-term, intermediate, and short-term goals. She always exudes this confidence and has a look on her face that says, "I can do it," every time we talk about medical science. She listens aptly whenever we talk, and I made her understand that achieving a goal is like building a house. I started by saying a house has many parts—the foundation, walls, roof, windows, doors, and more—and she nodded and said, "Yes, Aunty."

You must always take time to plan before embarking on any venture. I laid bare a sketchy map of the rigorous medical journey before Ayomide, not to scare her but to make her realise the discipline and diligence required not only to study medicine but also to be outstanding in all endeavours. I showed her she must properly lay her foundation.

It is your responsibility to find out what God wants you to do in life. Becoming outstanding in life requires planning, commitment, and tenacity or resolve to succeed on the pivot of hard work. In setting goals, you need to have a clear vision of where you want to go and how to get there.

It is also important to note that there is a huge difference between vision and ambition when setting goals. According to Bishop David Oyedepo, vision is our God-given purpose that we must find out, and ambition is our inner desire that we must strive to attain. The following table shows the differences between vision and ambition.

Vision	Ambition
This is God's original plan for you.	This is a self-set plan.
God must unfold the blueprint.	You must set the blueprint.
Divine direction is guaranteed when your anchor is God.	You create the path and direction.
You have the grace "ride", and you are unlikely to burn out.	You must run with God because by strength shall no man prevail.
You remain ever relevant, not outdated, as the Holy Ghost constantly updates, upgrades, and validates you.	You may sometimes struggle through if God is not with you.

What Strategy to Choose

After setting your goals, you need to have a clear strategy.

The strategy is the how, the process. The process sustains and keeps a dream or goal running. The process is what you do. The British English Dictionary defines *process* as "a series of actions or steps taken in order to achieve a particular end". What are your actions? What steps are you taking? The steps and actions you take that result in an excellent outcome are the process (not cutting corners or doing evil).

Process is what sustains what you do in life. When you succeed at what you do through a process of hard work, you will be able to sustain yourself at the top. You can always refine a process, but the basic principle of success is retained in the process. If you study and make good grades, the style that works for you is your process.

What is your strategy? Excellent results do not fall on people. There is always a price to pay to achieve that excellence. What price are you paying to achieve your goal? Do you read only when your examinations are close? Do you read from the minute you are taught so you can properly assimilate what you learn? Do you read when you should and do your assignments on time? Do you read ahead of the class, so that when you eventually cover the material in class, it is like revision? Do you study hard?

The American tennis player Serena Williams has been ranked the world's number-one female tennis champion for years. She has stayed on top of the league due to hard work. She does the hard work behind the scenes in the form of constant practice, exercising as a good strategy to defeat her opponents. Even what she eats is tailored to suit her body so she achieves success. She spends long hours training.

In the same way, Usain Bolt, the Jamaican athlete, won the men's one-hundred- and two-hundred-metre races in an unprecedented three straight Olympic games. That consistency earned him the nicknames "the world's fastest man" and "the fastest man alive". He had to undertake a lot of hard work involving long hours of training to get such outstanding success. Nothing pays like hard work born of a God-given idea set out with a good strategic plan. No success comes without hard work.

The ability to have everything in an instant is the advent of this digital age, which gives the impression that hard work is torture, or that hard work is stress! Hard work embodies the processes that make an

> Hard work is the cure to hard life.
>
> —Bishop David Abioye
>
> Hard work is actually the door to the high places of life.
>
> —Dr Paul Enenche and
> Dr Becky Enenche

individual learn and master strategies. Don't get me wrong, hard work does not mean an absence of failures or disappointments. However, when you fail, and you stand up again and again and again, the process of hard work makes you resilient and dogged, with the unflinching tenacity to face any storm in life.

When you bypass the process, you activate shortcuts, and it produces instant results, which others may applaud for a moment. However, when *real* storms come, you will implode or crash because you built your foundation on sand, not solid rock.

Everyone wants a good life. Everyone wants to spend money. Everyone wants to live in a nice house and own a fancy car as well. Everyone wants to belong to the haves and not to the have-nots.

How many are ready to pay the price of diligence? How many are ready for hard work?

The Bible expressly states that a faithful man shall abound with blessings, "but he that maketh haste to be rich shall not be innocent" (Proverbs 28:20). So have faithfulness in what you do. Don't cut corners; be diligent because "the hand of the diligent shall bear rule: but the slothful shall be under tribute" (Proverbs 12:24).

The Power of Focus in Achieving Your Set Goals

Focus is defined as the centre of activity or attraction (Merriam-Webster Dictionary). Focus is a powerful force in achieving your goals.

According to Merriam-Webster Dictionary, *focus* also means the following:

- "To concentrate on one thing intently in order to gain clarity"

- "To be totally committed to or be absorbed in a special assignment"

- "Ability to look unwaveringly at your purpose or assignment without distractions"

Pastor David Ibiyeomie says the following concerning focus:

- "No one ever gets anything worthwhile by accident. Life is all about focus."

- "Focus is individualistic not collective."

- "Focused people don't do good things, but they do the right things."

- "You only see obstacles when you take your eyes off your goal."

- "Staying focused in any given task is the main key to outstanding accomplishment."

- "Be focused because without focus nobody would know you."

- "Focused people are identified with something." What are you identified with?

- "People fail because of broken focus." May your focus never be broken!

You need to stay focused. Align with the outlined nuggets on focus, and see your life change for the better.

goal (with God) + focus = outstanding accomplishments

Have a work plan, and start from somewhere.

The following goal enablers could help you too:

- Push your goals—that is, pray until something happens (PUSH), till that vision comes to fruition (Proverbs 29:18).

- Keep proclaiming your plan; don't be quiet (James 3:10). Also, "a closed mouth is a closed destiny", as Bishop David Oyedepo says.

- Have a purpose (Proverbs 28:19)

- Stay focused (Philippians 3:14).

- Be persistent and diligent (Proverbs 6:6).

- Plan and replan your change strategy if necessary (Document your plans in a notebook with dates, and tick off things when they have come to pass.)

- Goal killers include the following:

- Prayerlessness

- Lack of planning

- Lack of commitment

- Laziness or slothfulness

- The sharing of your vision with the wrong persons

- Lack of extra effort to get extraordinary results

- An inability to manage time

- Social media addiction

You must set specific, measurable, attainable (or achievable), relevant, and time-bound (SMART) goals. If you see your existence as God's purpose and a project in God's hands with objectives and timelines, then you are on point. You can use the following SMART criteria as a guide *(Management Review,* George T. Doran, 1981).

- Make all your goals specific (on point).

- Set measurable goals.

- Let the goals be attainable or achievable.

- Make your goals relevant.

- Have time-bound timelines for attaining the set goals.

Many have set goals but have made mistakes in goal setting. According to Reverend Victor Adeyemi, mistakes of goal setting include the following:

- Lack of specificity

- Goals without recourse to God and current realities

- Goals without an execution plan

Action Points

- Have a reliable strategy to achieve your goal. Restrategize if your current strategy fails.

- Break down your goals into smaller plans that can fit into years, months, weeks, and days. Daily goals can be well managed. Accomplishing daily goals will give you a sense of fulfilment and ultimately lead you to achieve your bigger plans. Remember that a house is built little by little. I see you achieving all you set out to do in Jesus's name.

- Always stay focused.

- Be SMART!

- See you at the top!

> Any goal that is not given an appointment can never be fulfilled. A goal without a date is a wish.
>
> —The Catalyst
>
> Focus; otherwise, you will find life becomes a blur.
>
> —Anonymous
>
> Follow one course until successful.
>
> —Anonymous

Chapter 4: Time Management

Time management is crucial in everyone's life. But time is very challenging to define.

How would you define *time*? The Oxford English Dictionary defines time as the indefinite continued progress of existence and events in the past, present, and future regarded as a whole. Simply put, *time* makes us know which events have passed, are current, or yet to take place.

Time management is also life management. That means if you manage your time well, you manage your life well, and vice versa. Managing your time is important in achieving outstanding success, increased productivity, and amazing performance (Brian Tracy).

Do you use your time wisely, or do you waste it? Are you outstanding or lagging?

It is important to note that everything in life is associated with time. When you microwave food, for instance, depending on what type of food it is, you must time it, so you do not undercook, overcook, or even burn it. Time also defines success or failure. Nothing in life is timeless and endless except eternity. All things under heaven are timed. Appointments are kept with time in mind. Activities and plans are logged within time frames

Travel, for whatever reason—holiday travel, official travel, you name it—is a time-bound activity. So, apportioning time and sticking to it is an art that requires discipline, and a disciplined person is one who is in control of time. Remaining in control of time makes you soar. Lacking the ability to work with time may make you lose out on your destiny.

Are you in control of your time? How do you plan your day? What do your assign the most hours to?

Who owns your time?

Try this for a week: consciously note the time you spend on different activities, and draft a guide to planning your time. This will make you prioritise and learn how to do the hardest things first and possibly in bits.

In his book *Eat That Frog!*, Brian Tracy clearly states that there is nothing like "saving time" because everyone has 24 hours a day, 7 days a week, and 365 days a year. He further states that you can spend your time differently by doing tasks with higher value first. Some

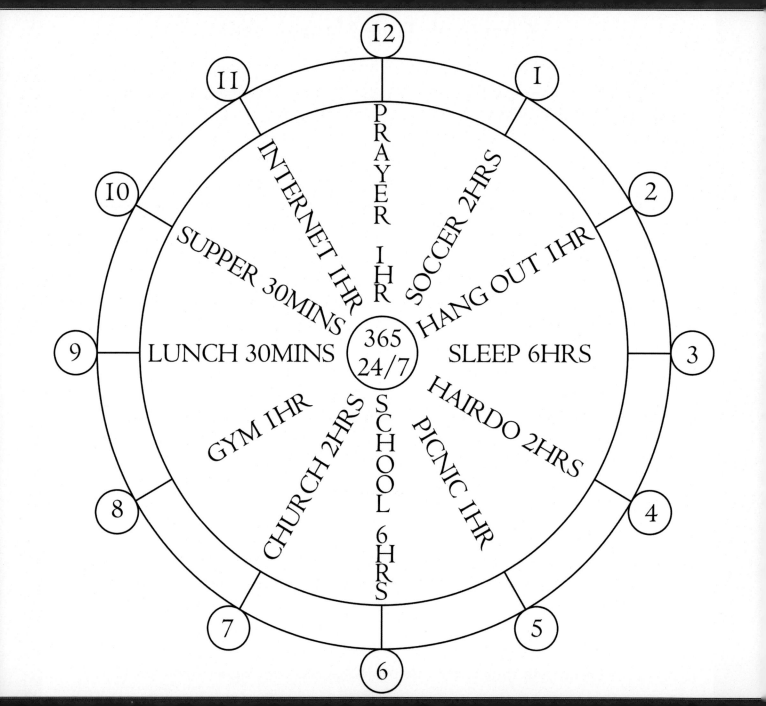

people are more outstanding in their endeavours than others because they "changed the order of their choices in the way they use time". Reorder your priorities by doing the hardest things first, and see how it changes your output. Put in little bits of effort towards your goal every day, and it will surely draw you closer to your target.

For instance, if you usually wake up late every day, you will find that many of your peers are far ahead of you in many areas. In reordering your choice to be the best, you must have the discipline to go to sleep early because "early to bed means early to rise" to accomplish your tasks. When you manage your time in a disciplined way, and do the hardest thing first, you will be on your way to greatness.

Write out the areas of your life you are struggling with, sketch a reordering plan with God's help, and stick to it. Stick to it for a day, a week, a month, and a year. After this time, you will discover that accomplishing a task on time has now become a habit. You will find out that with God's help, you shall form good time management habits. Someone once said, "If you are persistent, you will get it. If you are consistent, you will keep it." The keys here are persistence and consistency. Receive grace to have both.

I have encountered many teenagers and young adults who do not even know what to reorder! Consider this: if you find people complain that you are slow to commence a set task or activity, or you submit assignments late or never start anything early, it is a clue you have to reorder your priorities. That means managing your time wisely for excellent results.

When you value time, it means you place a premium on your destiny. "Time is money" is a popular cliché. Managing time is synonymous with managing money. No serious business person, for instance, would joke with time when it comes to purchasing goods or selling them to make a profit; all these activities are time bound. If you do any of them late or do not remain conscious of the time, your goods may expire, or you may lose great customers to competitors.

Do you have a plan? Your plan is the road map for your life! When you have a concrete, godly plan with timelines, and are bent on achieving it, you don't allow irrelevancies to sway or distract you because you have a checklist of activities to tick off. Having a plan indicates that you know where you are going. On the other hand, Bishop David Abioye said, "if you don't know where you are headed, everywhere would look like it." In saving your time, in the words of the German philosopher Goethe, "The things that matter most *must* never be at the mercy of things that matter least."

Action Points

- Have a plan.

- Reorder your plan if you are lagging behind in your assignments or targets.

- Be a stickler for time; don't run late for anything.

- Have an organizer. This could be a simple notebook where you write down your daily to-do list with timelines that you tick off when you accomplish items.

- When people know you stick to deadlines, you will earn their respect and achieve a lot in life.

- Ensure you have a daily deliverable sheet. *Don't* sleep until you have done something about what you planned for the day, as Frank Edward says.

- Admit your past mistakes, and move on.

- Face the future and move ahead; leave the past to pass with the past, as Bishop David Oyedepo says.

- Engage only in things with great benefits and rewards.

- The enemies of time are procrastination and your comfort zone. Identify these, and overcome them because "you don't have all the time in the world" (Lanre Olusola).

- Have a time chart on how long you expend energy and on what you expend it.

Resources

- *Time Management in an Instant* by Karen Leland and Keith Bailey

- *Eat That Frog!* by Brian Tracy

Time is useless without timeliness.

—Lanre Olusola

If you're going to be successful, pay attention to the way you use your time.

—Sam Adeyemi

Chapter 5: Choosing a Career Path

I have worked and mingled with pre-teens, teenagers, and young adults a lot, and what concerns me is how they choose a course of study in institutions of higher learning. A few months back, a ten-year-old girl walked up to me and asked, "Aunty, which profession pays more—medicine or engineering?"

For a split second, I said to myself, *What does this young girl need money for!*

She further added, "I want to be very rich and comfortable in life." The young want a life of luxury with utmost comfort, as does everyone. I sat the young girl down, and with God's help, I was able to explain to her that it is true "money answereth all things" but you must lay the foundation for making money well, and that takes a process. Everyone understands money makes life comfortable, and everyone loves the good life. Some teens and young adults want to make good money early in life, but the truth is "Hard work is the cure to hard labour and hard life" (Bishop David Abioye).

What reason will lead you to your choice of study? Money? Yes, money is very important, but is money the first reason? What is your passion? Have you identified your passions, skills, and talents? Everyone God created is wired with hidden skills and talents awaiting discovery.

Having passion for a course or career is paramount. When passion drives you, you will love what you do, and when you love what you do, you will remain dedicated to doing that. And in that process, before you know it, money will come. On the other hand, putting money first may lead to frustrations that have negative consequences. We live in a time when everyone wants to *hammer*, or be very successful financially. The Bible explicitly touches on this: "But he that maketh haste to be rich shall not be innocent" (Proverbs 28:20). We can't throw away the process of having financial success. The process authenticates and also sustains what one eventually ends up doing or achieving.

In choosing a course of study, you'll find different subjects that may fall into the following course categories—arts, sciences, social sciences, and so on. What you have a passion for will determine the right subject combination and eventually the right course. Whatever field of study you choose this way, you will prosper in it.

MEDICINE
LAW
ENGINEERING
PHARMACY
ARTS
BUSINESS
COMPUTER
? ?

Do not choose a course of study because your friends are doing the same. We are all wired differently. Don't be persuaded to do what you are not a natural for. The consequences will include struggles, frustrations, discontentment, and destiny derailment.

Having interfaced with youths, I have heard a few echo the following:

- "I was forced to read medicine and surgery, and as soon as I finish, I will hand the degree to my dad and face business."

- "Because my parents wanted their land dispute settled well, they felt an in-house lawyer was a great idea; they coaxed me into reading law."

- "You know, my father has a big business empire, and he feels since I am his first son, studying business administration is just perfect. I don't like business administration."

- "I was too young to know what I wanted, and my parents could not guide me either since they were not educated. I just read geography and regional planning. I wish I followed my passion and read pharmacy."

I heard the preceding statements at different times, and they all caused me great concern. Many people want and chase after titles (*doctor*, *engineer*, b*arrister*, a*rchitect*, s*urveyor*, e*state surveyor*—the list is endless!). These titles in and of themselves are not bad; if they match God's calling for you, they are good. However, if God did not create you to have them, they would become a burden, and every day would be full of regrets. Every course of study is good! Find your path, set the pace, and soar. Wrongly chasing titles, in the words of Bishop David Oyedepo, "leave[s] one without entitlements".

How to Choose a Career

This very important decision will shape the rest of your career, life, and destiny. Keep these points in mind when choosing a career:

- Knowing God, hearing Him, and having a personal relationship with Him make it easy to know what He created you for.

- Find out about your proposed course, ask questions, and even research it.

- Have godly academic mentors if possible.

- Some schools have guidance or career counsellors; seek their advice as well.

- What are your strengths? What subjects are you good at? Stick to your strengths. *Don't* struggle with weaknesses; you will shine more and more at the point of strength.

- Prayerfully discuss your passion with your parents.

- Hillary Clinton once said, "Follow your heart and not conventions," in choosing a career. I say to you to follow your passion, not what the crowd chases or what "sells". God wired you for a purpose. Find out what the purpose is in His book the Bible.

Have the correct subject combination: arts, sciences, social sciences, and so on. Ask questions. It is better to ask many questions than to not make enquiries and miss your way.

Career Nuggets

Things to pay attention to when choosing a career:

- Even if you have a talent that can spin millions of dollars per minute, I advise that you get educated (get a degree, diploma, or whichever certification); education broadens your thinking and may help polish you so you can better deliver and fulfil your vision. Also know that the talent (or gift) God has bestowed on you will make a way for you (Proverbs 18:16). Be educated in your field, prepared, and always willing to learn.

- You need diligence to achieve unparalleled success. When you have diligence in what you do, you shall stand before kings and not mean men (Proverbs 22:29). You require diligence to finish whatever you start. *Don't* drop out of school for any reason. Winners don't quit! In whatever you have the talent to do, diligence, hard work, and focus are key ingredients to fulfil your purpose. You cannot be a winner if you are good at what you do but you lack diligence, or you are hardworking but not focused. We live in a competitive world, and you must have sound thinking and "know your onions" to stand out and reach the top. There is no space for sluggards at the top. If you make *diligence and hard work* your watchword, you will permanently remain at the top.

- Don't despise little beginnings. Your beginning may be a struggle, but you are not permitted to live and end life that way. Start small and grow *big*.

- Develop the ability to spot distractions. Stay focused to achieve your dreams.

- Align your course with your passion.

- Sometimes, your course and passion will not align. Later in life, you may discover that you have a career and a passion. But the passion could serve as your business that you earn money from.

- Do a lot of research on your proposed course of study, and if possible, meet with godly mentors in the field to make an informed decision. Don't rush into university under the cliché of "time is going or far spent". If you just pick any course of study, when you graduate, you will only be frustrated.

- Learn a skill. This is an especially good thing to do during holidays or when you are through with secondary school and awaiting university admission. Nobody is born empty. I know a young adult male named Ayo, who is a law student at a Nigerian university. He makes very lovely knapsacks, notepads, and customized bags from Ankara (an African print used to make different kinds of fabrics) during vacations and makes good money selling them. When I interviewed him to find out how he got into the business, he said this:

In a world where our generation is looking for free meals and depending on our parents for survival … there comes a time we will be left alone to take life struggles alone when they are gone. … Life will only give you what you earn, not what you wish.

Ayo is focused and already an entrepreneur while still an undergraduate.

Talent

Your talent is also important; harness it. Your talent is your natural expertise or skill that God deposited in you. When you engage it, you deliver results effortlessly, without stress and on point. God endowed you with this gift that would make you stand before kings and not mean men.

When I encourage teens to draft or sketch their post-graduation plans, I usually pose this question: "When you graduate from university with that degree, and there are no immediate white-collar jobs, what plans do you have in place to survive legally?" That brings our discussion to plan B.

Talking about talents, what are you good at? What can you do effortlessly and so passionately that you must be stopped? What is that thing that wows people when you engage in it? Is there a meeting point for your career and talent?

God deposited something in you when He created you because He created nobody empty. Some of these gifts or talents can be harnessed early if you identify them. A typical African example is Kareem Waris Olamilekan, a Nigerian making waves with his hyperrealistic drawings. He started drawing at age six and now gets worldwide recognition. You are the next to be recognised.

How to Find Your Talent

Consider the following when determining your talent:

- People may point you to your talent, always referring to how good you are in a particular area or thing.

- Your talent may be what you enjoy most.

- Your talent may be what you do easily with amazing results.

Pay attention to that talent. It may involve painting, drawing, designing fashion, catering—whatever, when developed, can fetch money someday. Build on it!

> There are no limits to what you can accomplish except the limits you place on your own thinking.
>
> —Brian Tracy
>
> You get rewarded for your results and not your efforts.
>
> —Sam Adeyemi
>
> If you can imagine it, you can create it. If you can dream it, you can become it.
>
> —William Ward

Chapter 6: Puberty in Boys

Puberty in young boys involves hormone-controlled changes that take place in their bodies and gradually transform them into full-grown men.

Changes in boys include the following:

- Enlargement of the reproductive organs
- The breaking of the voice
- Pubic, axillary (armpit), and facial hair growth

The hormone testosterone controls all these things—the reproductive organs (the testes, scrotum, and penis) enlarging, the voice breaking, and the hair growing at different places. The voice breaks because the action of hormones on the vocal cord and voice box makes boys speak deeply (with a bass or baritone voice) so they perfectly fit their God-given function. Hair grows in different places just the way God designed it, and this may require shaving powder or a shaving stick.

This phase may be quite challenging for some young men, especially those who also have to deal with acne (or pimples). A few young men also grow very worried at their nocturnal emissions, which people generally refer to as *wet dreams*. These are harmless emissions. You need to know that God made you special, and all of the above experiences are meant to transform you into a functional God-fearing adult, ready to do His will and change the world for His glory. You were perfectly designed.

Further tips for young men include the following:

- Own your hair clippers, and *do not* share them with friends
- Avoid tight inner clothing (Cotton boxers are recommended.)
- Regularly wash your boxers
- Use deodorants and perfumes

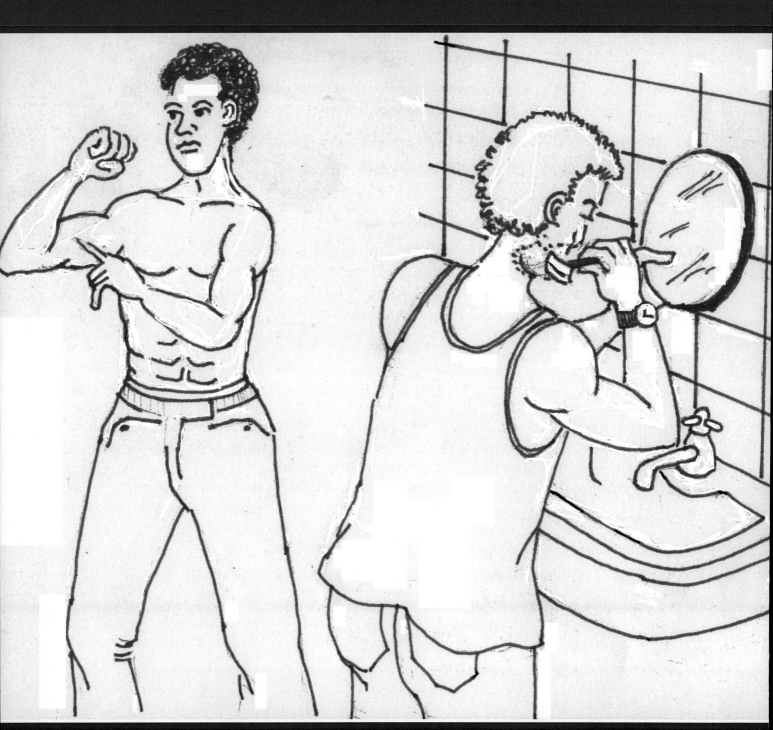

Action Points

- Bathe regularly to prevent body odour.

- Shave regularly.

- Regularly check to ensure the two small testes are in the God-ordained sac (or scrotum) and hang outside the body. If not found this way, you may have an undescended testis; discuss this with your parents, and seek medical attention as soon as possible.

- If your scrotum sometimes swells (maybe due to hydrocele) and also occasionally feels painful, discuss it with your parents, and seek urgent medical attention.

Chapter 7: Puberty in Girls

The process of sexual development known as *puberty* makes children into adolescents capable of reproducing sexually (British English Dictionary). The puberty stage acts as a bridge one must cross to get to adulthood. Boys and girls start puberty at different times, and even those of the same age or sex will experience its onset differently.

The whole process of puberty starts in the brain, and it is controlled by hormones. The brain releases these hormones to different parts of the body and effects changes in boys and girls as programmed by God (Genesis 1:27). Just as the parts of a car have different functions (the car seat is for sitting, the steering wheel for navigating, and the tyres for propelling the car), so do the parts of the body have different functions, as you shall see shortly.

The changes in girls during puberty follow this order:

- Breast enlargement (thelarche)

- Pubic and axillary (armpit) hair growth (pubarche)

- Menstruation (menarche)

- Acne (or pimples) development

Breast enlargement is the first pubertal sign to occur, and the breasts keep growing throughout puberty and beyond. No two girls have the same size of breasts. When the breasts are initially budding, "training bras" are recommended to keep the breasts firm and fit when girls wear clothes. As the breasts grow bigger, their brassiere size will change.

During the pubic and axillary hair development (pubarche) phase, hairs grow in the armpits and the genital area popularly known as the *private part*. Some adolescents have more hair than others do in these areas, and thus, they tend to sweat more and may even need to shave these areas with their mothers' help. Due to excessive sweat during puberty, frequent bathing and use of deodorant is highly recommended.

Menstruation, or the commencement of menses, is also known as *menarche*. In simple terms, this means the shedding of an unfertilised egg, which comes out through the vagina as blood. Many research studies have shown that black people start menses two to four years earlier than white people. And recently, in medical practice, we have increasingly seen young girls start menstruating from the age of eight. The menstrual cycle occurs every month in adolescent girls. The hormone progesterone controls this process.

Other parlance for *menstruation* includes *period*, *being on*, and *my time*. It is sometimes very disturbing when young girls don't keep records of their monthly menstruation. It is necessary that you keep a diary of your monthly periods or menses so you record them accurately. (Mark from the date the period starts to its last day.) This will help you know the pattern the menstrual cycle takes. No two young girls have the same menstrual cycle. For some people, the menstrual cycle comes every eighteen days, while for others, it could arrive every twenty-one to forty-two days. Infrequent menstruation or delayed periods may require medical attention. It is worthy of mention that very few adult women have never menstruated. Recording your menstruation monthly is very important so, if the menstrual cycle changes—for example, due to irregularities, delays, or cessation of menses—you can easily detect it early. Also some girls may have heavy or excessive flow with clots or a longer-than-usual duration of flow; they need a gynaecological expert to sort this out and advise them accordingly.

I have seen teenage girls in clinics who had gynaecological issues, and I have talked with some of them one-on-one. Some of them never knew what a menstrual cycle was. Some had no menstrual records, yet they never considered that menstrual delays were real issues that need medical attention. Some only realised in marriage that they had baseline gynaecological issues that may delay conception.

Premenstrual Syndrome (PMS)

A few days before menstruation, some young girls and women may become a bit irritable, moody, angry, or just generally low. Such mood swings regularly occur and form what is popularly called *PMS* or *premenstrual tension*. This is sometimes characterized by headaches, irritability, breast tenderness or pain, abdominal cramps, fatigue, bouts of anger, and loss of appetite. Eating a balanced diet, exercising, and taking warm baths really helps during this time.

Acne

Acne or pimples come with puberty and can be quite distressing and troublesome. For some teenagers, acne gets worse shortly before and during the menstrual period. Acne generally wanes after the teenage years, although some adults may have breakouts from time to time.

Breast Self-Examination

As a teenage or young adult girl, it is important you know how to do a breast self-examination to detect breast lumps early and also recognise alarm signs, if any. The steps are as follows:

1. A week after your menses, stand in front of a good mirror, and raise your hands upwards and forwards with your brassiere off. Look at your breasts' symmetry, size, shape, and colour; check whether both are the same or they have changed any. Is one breast bigger than the other? Naturally, many females have one breast that is slightly bigger than the other, but when the size difference is very remarkable, and possibly painful, you may need to see a doctor.

2. Check for breast discharge by gently milking the breasts (gently pressing from the base of the breast to the nipple). If either breast or both breasts express milk when you are not pregnant, it calls for medical attention.

3. Check for any lump (*breast mouse*) by dividing each breast into four equal quadrants (that is, into four equal parts). In an anticlockwise fashion, gently check from quadrant to quadrant with the tips of all four fingers. If you feel anything unusual (like a tiny seed in any of the quadrants, which may be a lump), consult your doctor.

4. Examine your axilla (armpit), and run your finger down your armpit (or axillary tail), checking for any tiny seeds (known as *breast lymph nodes*) if present.

Doing regular monthly checks, especially a week after your menses, is recommended. Regular breast examinations have saved many due to early detection of a breast abscess, discharge, or a lump. As a child of God, no evil shall befall you.

Action Points

- Do monthly breast self-exams to check for early signs of breast lumps. Breast lumps may need excision if present.

- Bathe more often during your menses, and regularly change your sanitary pads to reduce body odour.

- Record your periods monthly and accurately. You can record these in a handwritten diary or, alternatively, with a period-recording smartphone app. Store these records, retrieve them, and upload them to your doctor when the need arises. Keeping these records helps detect delayed or irregular menstruation early.

- Consult your mother and seek medical attention if you have delayed, scanty, frequent, or irregular periods.

- It is important to note that some full-grown women have never menstruated. Seek urgent medical attention if you are old enough to but have never menstruated.

- Learn to manage PMS as recommended.

- Troublesome acne can lead to an inferiority complex and low self-esteem. Consult a dermatologist about acne.

Resources

- Maurer Foundation for Breast Health Education

- *The Bible Cure for PMS and Mood Swings* by Don Colbert, MD

- *Growing Up God's Way for Girls* by Dr Chris Richards and Dr Liz Jones

- *Raising Godly Children* by Faith A. Oyedepo

Chapter 8: You and Your Sexuality

Sex is one of the most used and abused words for several reasons. Our world is saturated with different sexual messages. Sex is a strong force, and as a youth, you need to know God's plan and purpose concerning sex. Scripturally and morally, it is an act exclusively reserved for the married, as God designed it (Harold J. Sala). However, the enemy has used and is still using it as a tool to destroy men's destiny.

This digital era—with the partially censored and uncensored sex messages on the Internet and all forms of social media—makes the teenage phase more challenging. But feel confident that "There hath no temptation taken you but that such as is common to man: but God is faithful, who will not suffer you to be tempted above that ye are able; but will with the temptation also make a way to escape, that ye may be able to bear it" (1 Corinthians 10:13).

It is important to know that God demands that we be holy as He is holy (1 Peter 1:16).

Teenagers are very inquisitive. Some are adventurous and outgoing, and others are overtly reserved and quiet. I must say the teenage years can challenge people, with the different temperaments and personalities evolving and with the hormones finding expression. Also, the different developmental stages of this phase can prove uneventful for some and pure exploration and adventure for others. Teens may exhibit moody, excited, expressionless, attention-seeking, or acceptance-seeking behaviour. Sometimes, teens have also experienced the following:

- Wanted others to notice them

- Wanted to outdo and outshine others

- Wanted freedom of expression

- Wanted to belong

- Demanded what is their right

- Wanted to be treated like adults

- Demanded respect

- Had crushes on or felt infatuated with others

Some may want to start dating, while others who are sexually active may misinterpret sex to mean love!

These are real feelings and real issues. It does not make you abnormal if you have a crush, but the actions that follow the crush or infatuation can lead you to sin. Keep in mind there is time for everything. You were made in God's image, and the whole duty of man is to serve God and keep His commandments. God placed in you the capacity to love and show love, and by that, I mean God's kind of love, the agape love. Learning self-control and really being controlled by God at this phase is crucial. Arousing erotic love at this phase is destructive.

It really pains me when I hear about young teenagers partying all night and doing things unworthy of mention. I have been privileged to work with teenagers, and I have seen teenagers who lost their virginity, uterus, and ovaries (their complete womb) while "enjoying life". I have also managed many youths on HIV drugs, and a few who have been hepatitis B positive. Sadly, these diseases are sexually transmitted and preventable! Some have died of all of these. I have heard teens say the following statements several times:

- "Aunty, my friends have all deserted me. … They say I am a *Jew* [local parlance for a naïve person]."

- "Everyone is doing it."

- "I have to *test* ['have sex'] to see whether I am fertile, before my marriage years."

- "My boyfriend would leave me if don't *sleep* ['have sex'] with him."

- "I am not a bad person. I don't do all those bad things. … I only masturbate when the urge comes. At least I am not having sex."

Following God and walking with Him is a personal decision. "Serving God is not a gift, it is a choice" (Bishop David Oyedepo). When you decide to follow God wholeheartedly and sincerely, you will have grace there to carry you through and keep you.

Have you ever said any of the preceding quoted statements, or have you ever done or gotten involved in any of the described actions? You are not alone. Many have gone that way, living in pretence and falsehood to belong to a certain popular group. That is not the way to go. Get it straight; sin is sin no matter what others call it.

Current research findings have revealed an increase in early sexual debuts among preteens. An early sexual debut does a lot to your spiritual mind and your physical body. It erodes your self-confidence, reduces your self-esteem and self-worth, and puts you in the bondage of sexual sin for as long as you live in it. It also exposes you to the very high risk of incurable sexually transmitted infections. Physically, these cause you to die slowly while awaiting eternal condemnation if you do not repent. You don't need to be sexually exposed or active to make it in life. You were bought for a price, so God's got your back; you are a star! I pray that you will be willing and obedient.

Masturbation is not the way out, and not the way to go either; it is self-arousal, and I bet you feel a sense of guilt after such an act, unless your heart is hardened already. Sex, as God designed it, is to be expressed in marriage unreservedly. Your main duty at this phase is to focus on your studies, plan for your admirable future, make an impact in life, set the pace, become a trailblazer, raise the bar of academic achievement, and create indelible landmarks in your course of choice or area of endeavour. There is no doubt that early involvement in sexual sin derails you from your destiny and ends in frustrations. The Amplified Bible clearly states that there is a season for everything and a time for every delight, event, or purpose under heaven (Ecclesiastes 3:1). Now is the time to study and strive to be outstanding!

No deviant, adamant, and unrepentant teenage behaviour ends well. Every naïve teenager, in wanting to belong, ends up consumed and destroyed by this behaviour. A popular saying says, "As you make your bed, so you must lie on it"; make your "bed" with Christ so you can lie well without crisis and stress. Get your emotions under control with God's help. With God's help, constantly and consciously channel your urges and emotions into positive, constructive activities.

Any ungodly things you read, meditate on, and feed on can dangerously arouse your sexual desires to unquenchable levels.

You are the author of your destiny. Sin does not fall on people! It starts with a thought that crystallizes into action. However, at the thought level, you can stop it, and I see you stopping it in Jesus's name! No teenager can effectively handle the teenage phase and please God in this era without Christ. Let Christ be your anchor, and you are good to go. I love this illustration.

> teenager + Christ = salvation, divinity, and freedom from sin

> teenager – Christ = crisis, no self-control, and condemnation

Teens have loads of energy, which they must channel appropriately. Do the following to handle the teenage-years fireworks:

- Have Christ in your life, and be born again. Have a personal relationship with God when not doing religion; that will help you channel your energy aright in crushing evil thoughts and actions.

- Only love for God will maintain your heart and mind through the teenage phase and beyond.

- Always surround yourself with prayers.

- Be bold and confident, and have a positive self-image.

- Learn to say no, not in rebellion but in godliness.

- Have a daily memory verse; meditate on it.

- Attend a Bible-believing church or fellowship, and actively maintain your fire for God.

- Set personal but godly principles early in life—for example, having no sex before marriage, dressing in decent ways, choosing godly friends and company, and saying no to every appearance of evil. Don't conform to the world's standards (Romans 12:1–2).

- Manage your emotions under God. Tell God about them; talk to your parents. Crush that crush by channelling your energy into positive things—such as writing, evangelising, building up your faith by reading godly books, learning a skill, and watching godly and inspiring movies—to keep you on track.

- Discuss your fears and feelings with your parents. Crushes and infatuations are temporary feelings; if not well handled, they can defeat you and derail you from your academics and your God-given and amiable destiny. When you start having butterflies and feelings of love about the opposite sex, ask yourself, "Where would this lead me at this time?" There is time for everything. If you start exploring erotic love—and all that has to do with it—when you should instead be studying, you are playing with fire, and it will soon burn you. Many have gotten pregnant and fathered children they were not ready for. Consciously talk to God about your crush. Tame your emotions by transferring your energy to God. Meditate on positive things to avoid getting further sucked into evil and thereby falling from grace. I see you standing tall for Christ. You, too, shall overcome *and* mentor others.

- Before entering any relationship, ask these questions (Pastor Jerry Eze):

    o Is it right?

    o Is the time right?

o   Is my heart right?

Action Points

- Don't live other people's lives; live your own life with no pretence.

- Bond with your parents; be their friends so you can discuss issues that bother you with your parents and get their good counsel.

- Channel your energy into planned positive activities.

- Keep godly company. Not everyone you come across should eventually become your friend.

- Immediately report to your church teachers and your parents if anything goes wrong (for example, rape).

- Maintain a decent dress code, not unduly exposing your body (Romans 12:1–2). "The way you dress is the way you would be addressed" (Bishop David Oyedepo). If you expose your private areas, people will address you as a prostitute; if unkempt, you will be addressed as a tout. Dress responsibly to command honour and respect.

> Undefined relationships are risky.
>
> —Pastor Jerry Eze

- There is time for everything (Ecclesiastes 3:17). You have time for studying, marrying,

> Sex is medicine and marriage is the prescription. If you're not married you're taking an illegal drug.
>
> —Pastor Jerry Eze

and having children. Focus on building up your life at this stage to make a mark in your generation.

- Define your friendships!

Resources

- *Dating: A Biblical Guide* by Faith A. Oyedepo

- *Train Up a Child and Be Glad You Did* by Harold J. Sala

Chapter 9: Your Health, Your Responsibility

Everyone should cherish celebrating life with those who have lived it well. I was invited to the birthday party of Pa Gabriel Adeyinka, a ninety-seven-year-old man, early this year in South-West Nigeria. In attendance were his children, his grandchildren, and a few great-grandchildren, family friends, and friends. The birthday started with a church service and ended with an after-party.

Pa Adeyinka's party was not the usual kind of party because it included different lectures on different burning life issues. He danced and thrilled the audience, could read without glasses, had an intact memory, and walked straight without a walking stick or aid. He could pass for someone in his sixties, with his clean shave. After he cut his impressive cake, the moment everyone was waiting for came, when he shared the secret of his youthful, ageless look and brilliance, after lots of side talks about his looks, strength, and energy at ninety-seven years old.

The celebrant told the audience that the secret of his staying healthy and strong was getting it right from the beginning. He had known the Lord from age twelve, when a missionary led him to Christ, and ever since, the Lord had been with him. Having the fear of the Lord from early in life and staying on track with the Lord had shielded him from different vices. He also emphasized he watched what he ate and exercised regularly. My takeaway from that party was the title of this chapter.

The beginning is now.

When you truly serve the Lord, He services you and keeps you alive for longer because stones would not serve the Lord. Serving the Lord without conditions prolongs your life, according to Dr Paul Enenche. How committed are you to kingdom service? The men and women who knew and served the Lord as teens and are now adults have constantly reiterated that it pays to serve the Lord, and their destinies have been decorated in the process.

Is it possible to be in health?

The Bible says, "Beloved, I wish above all things that thou mayest prosper and be in health, even as thy soul prospereth" (3 John 1:2). As a child of God, divine health is your right. But

you need to know what to do to get it right. "My people are gone into captivity, because they have no knowledge: and their honourable men are famished, and their multitude dried up with thirst" (Isaiah 5:13).

Do you do anything about your health? Are you comfortable with your weight and looks? Do you eat in the right proportions, or do you overindulge and have obesity? The World Health Organization defines *health* as a state of complete physical, mental, and social well-being, and not merely the absence of disease or infirmity.

Examples of people who lived a long time include the following:

- Moses (for 120 years)

- Simeon (as stated in Luke 2:29–30)

- Jesus (who was never sick)

In our generations, many have lived and are still living a long time. You have a responsibility towards your health. What you do daily in keeping healthy eventually becomes your habit (Mike Murdock). If you cultivate a healthy habit early and stick to it, it will have many rewards, one of which is a long life. We all pray to live long. That is good, but we also must work at it because faith without works is dead. Remember you need to do it right from the beginning, first giving your life to Christ at an early age. That is the beginning.

Eating right is crucial to the lifelong responsibility of being healthy. The body needs nutrients from different food types for the cells, tissues, organs, and systems to function well and fight diseases. A balanced diet should consist of proteins (bodybuilding blocks), carbohydrates (energy-giving nutrients), fats (healthy fats), and vitamins and minerals in the right quantities for excellent growth.

It is advisable that you take more natural drinks, like smoothies. Drink local drinks like *kunu* (made from millet), *zobo* (made from roselle leaves), *kunu aya* (made from tiger nuts), or any local drink in your community. These are richer in nutrients and also healthier than fizzy drinks.

Exercise is important because it helps the body function well and keep fit, apart from its other numerous benefits. Most schools, from kindergarten to secondary school, incorporate it into their curricula because of its importance.

In the contemporary world, TV and Internet adverts most times feature beautiful light-skinned ladies (known as *slay queens*) and men with six-packs as models. You need to understand that these models are trained, and over time, they develop a routine to maintain that physique. In the quest to belong as slay queens, many young girls literally starve themselves to achieve the *figure 8* shape, and I constantly hear statements like "Aunty, I wear a UK size 8," and "I want to look like ABC and XYZ." The *role model syndrome*, as I call it, is really a challenge. It has ruined many teenagers; in trying to be like their role models, many hit the extreme with grave consequences. For the young men, bodybuilding is it. These bodybuilding exercises involve an exceptionally high-protein diet to attain the six-pack look. In the words of Nike Adeyemi, "As you slay your body, also slay your spirit to be in tune and right standing with God."

Many youths have starved themselves over time, and ended up malnourished and with gastric ulcers. Sadly, a few boys engaging in bodybuilding have fallen flat backwards, hit their heads on the floor, and sustained fractures of the cervical vertebrae, resulting in arm and leg paralysis. Exercise with caution.

It is important to know that some youths have been diagnosed with hypertension, diabetes, obesity, and even sickle cell anaemia. Knowing your health status, you need to take responsibility for your health early in order to live long. God is faithful to giving you a long life. However, not taking responsibility for your health is irresponsible.

Youths frequently ask me what their ideal weight is. I want to state that your ideal weight is a function of your height. You can have a healthy weight by eating right and eating food in the right proportion.

To determine your ideal or target weight, the body mass index (BMI)—which is a categorization of how much weight you carry compared with your height—is very important. The ideal BMI is 18.5 – 25 kg/m^2. Per the World Health Organization standards, you may calculate your ideal weight by multiplying the ideal BMI with the square of your

height (in metres). Thus, if your height is 1.75 metres, your ideal weight will be between $18.5 \times 1.75^2 = 56.7$ kilograms and $25 \times 1.75^2 = 76.6$ kilograms (https://bit.ly/2F7XVwx).

BMI is interpreted differently in teens than in adults. The interpretations of these weight status categories determine your category and what you should do to maintain a healthy weight. Consult your doctor if you are underweight, overweight, or obese, as each has its negative consequences.

Action Points

- Know your BMI to ascertain your weight category.

- Eat a daily balanced diet (with carbohydrates, protein, vitamins, minerals, and so on), and avoid junk food.

- Drink natural drinks (such as *zobo*, which is made from roselle leaves; *kunu aya*, which is a tiger nut drink; and smoothies).

- Do not consciously skip meals, except when you are fasting, for weeks in order to avoid anorexia, peptic ulcers, and so on.

- Be very careful when doing muscle-building exercises.

- Know your genotype. Do not wait till you are about to get married before getting a test. Ensure you get a confirmatory test using advanced testing methods such as HPLC especially in Africa.

- Know your blood group.

- Know your hepatitis B and C status; if it's negative, take the appropriate vaccine.

- Know your HIV status; if it's positive, see a doctor for further counselling and care.

- Note and know your allergies, if you have any.

- Have your eyes regularly checked for early detection of any eye condition.

- Discuss any medical issue with your parents, and seek medical attention early.

- Have an annual comprehensive check-up. Get your blood pressure and blood sugar checked, especially if either of your parents is hypertensive or diabetic. Recently, the numbers of juvenile diabetics and hypertensives have increased.

- Pray, as good health is your right in Christ.

Additional tips for healthy living include the following:

- Frequently bathe with soap and water, especially during menses.

- Wash and condition your hair at least once a month. Do not leave your hair unkempt in order to avoid hair lice and dandruff.

- Own your pedicure and manicure set; do not share blades and other sharp instruments.

- Get your own needles; if you must fix your hair, *do not* reuse needles!

- Get your own towels for salon use.

- Get your own nail polish; use nail hardener if you must paint your fingernails or toenails.

- Get or buy your own nail polish remover; *do not* share.

- Sun-dry shoes you have worn over time, especially in the tropics.

- Endeavour to sun-dry pants and other underwear, and go the extra mile to iron your pants if possible.

- Avoid tight clothing, especially tight underwear, in tropical environments because that promotes the growth of *Candida albicans*, which causes candidiasis. Most people wrongly refer to this as *toilet disease*. In fact, some sexually transmitted infections are also wrongly labelled as toilet diseases. What young girls and older women wrongly refer to as *toilet disease* is most often diagnosed as candidiasis, which is a fungal infection.

Predisposing factors of candidiasis include the following:

- Wearing tight underwear (The tropics especially encourage the growth of the yeast candida and promote its multiplication.)

- Douching (This involves washing and irrigating the vagina with water. Douching to a point that it distorts the vagina's normal flora makes the vagina susceptible to infections. For example, it may lead to a yeast infection, which causes candida.)

- Overusing antibiotics

- Suppressing the immune system due to diabetes, HIV, cancers, medications such as steroids and other immune system–suppressing drugs, and so on

Symptoms of candidiasis include the following:

- Intense itching around the vagina

- Whitish discharge from the vagina

Avoid candidiasis in the following ways:

- Avoid tight underwear.

- Avoid every other listed predisposing factor.

Also note

- See your doctor if you have any form of vaginal discharge; do not self-medicate.

- There is a popular saying that cleanliness is next to godliness. As you keep your body clean, watch that you also keep the spirit clean.

Chapter 10: Dealing With Body Odour

Ada was a plump eleven-year-old girl who had a characteristic dimple when she smiled. She had just gotten into secondary school in Abuja, Nigeria. Filled with the excitement of starting this phase of life's journey, and being purely sanguine, she was always joyful, easily made friends, and interacted nicely. However, she repeatedly noticed that when in her friends' company, conversations did not last long, and a few times, some friends winced and covered their noses when in her presence. This made Ada worried and withdrawn, which affected her academics. Her childhood friend, Anita, who was a student in the same school but not the same class, summoned the courage to tell Ada about her body odour and advised her to talk to her parents and seek medical help.

Do you find yourself in Ada's situation?

This is a very sensitive issue, and it is also not so easy to walk up to someone and say, "You have body odour." It is essential to know that body odour has ruined healthy friendships. However, someone may have body odour and not know it; others may know it but not exactly know how to tackle it. Body odour sometimes results from poor hygiene. But body odour has varied causes, and some people usually experience it for the first time as they become teenagers or young adults.

There are many causes of body odour. A sound knowledge of the following underlying causes would make tackling some of them easy:

- Sweating in hairy areas causes body odour; bacteria subsequently act on the sweat, resulting in body odour. This may be the most common cause of odour.

- Not bathing well or even washing the private parts well (for example, during ladies' menses) causes body odour.

- Certain people's systems cannot completely break down compounds into odourless chemicals, which can be excreted in their urine or sweat. When these incompletely broken-down chemicals are present in the urine, sweat, or breath, it can result in body odour. These compounds may be produced from seafood and *offal* (the entrails or inner parts of an animal). In Nigeria, offal is popularly known as *shaki, intestines,* or *roundabout* in local parlance.

- When diabetics have poor sugar control, they may have acetone breath and fish-like odour oozing out of them.

- Prolonged shoe wearing results in an unpleasant odour among people with fungal infections, especially of the feet.

- Other medical conditions, like dripping urine or leaking urine and faeces, can produce bad body odour too.

Action Points

- Avoid seafood and offal.

- If you have a sugar issue, get your sugar under control, as this goes a long way towards controlling the odour.

- Treat any underlying fungal infection to resolve the odour.

- Some medical conditions may require treating the underlying causes, which in most cases may involve medical or surgical interventions.

- As a young person, body odour can make your friends desert you, and in our society, not many people may be bold enough to tell their friends that they have body odour. Make personal hygiene a habit. Follow the popular saying that cleanliness is next to godliness.

- Bathe regularly—at least twice a day (in the morning and evening)—and use a good deodorant and a mild perfume. These go a long way towards dousing the odour.

Always have a small perfume with you, especially if you sweat a great deal. However, do not use perfumes to replace or substitute for bathing regularly.

Always have a small perfume with you, especially if you sweat a great deal.

Chapter 11: Addiction

We live in an era of super cravings. We may crave God, TV shows, games, honest friendships, relationships, and more. We all need something or someone to lean on, an unquestionable assurance. Man, by nature, tries to satisfy many cravings, whether or not they're godly. Addiction glues people to a thing. Anything or any substance that can be consumed in some form and that makes one high can be abused, and this leads to addiction.

Human beings are spirits who have a soul and live in a body (1 Thessalonians 5:23). And they totally depend on God as their anchor. Now it is crucial that young men and women know the Lord at an early age, so the Lord becomes their anchor in life.

If you lack God as an anchor, you will naturally tend to derail or slip from God's presence. Man, if not anchored to God, will by nature find an anchor in something other than God. If teens or young adults do not find succour or solace in God, then they will find an anchor in someone or something else. Young people sometimes end up finding this anchor that is not God Almighty in an addiction that they have exposure to. They may develop this addiction because of negative peer pressure.

What are your honest answers to the following questions?

- Where is your anchor?

- What or where do you draw your energy from when you need to double your efforts?

- What do you fall back on when you feel frustrated or overwhelmed?

- Who and what do you depend on for extra confidence when you need to deliver?

- What makes you "high"?

- Who do you associate with? Does the company you keep derail you?

"Your association determines your level of accomplishments," someone once said. What can you accomplish if you are addicted to something?

Even though you may graduate as a first-class student, CEO, successful entrepreneur, or employer of labour later in life, if you are a slave to something other than God, you will never have contentment in life. Mike Murdock said, "The secret of your success is found in your daily routine." What is your daily routine?

The American Psychiatric Association defines *addiction* as a "disorder because of the repeated desire to satisfy self despite the grave consequences". Most people are familiar with drug addiction. However, in the past decade or more, various other addictions have also affected teens. These include the following:

- Substance abuse (used interchangeably with *drug abuse* or *addiction*)

- Food addiction (which can lead to obesity)

- Sexual addiction

- Behavioural addiction

- Computer addiction

- Social media addiction

- Pornography addiction

Causes of addiction include the following:

- Negative peer pressure and bad company

- A dysfunctional background

- A lack of parental supervision

- Repeated failure in school

- Negative self-image

- Low self-esteem

- The environment

- Domestic violence

- Childhood neglect

All addictions have a root cause. Some addicts are products of out-of-wedlock or broken marriages or even unbalanced homes. Permissive parenting, where parents do not firmly discipline their children, has also resulted in teenage addicts. In addition, a lack of confidence and love, as well as repeated failure in school, has been found to cause addiction. The environment or neighbourhood where teens grow up can also hugely influence them.

For others, addiction is a revenge mission to get back at their parents, an adventurous phase, or just a personal decision to behave defiantly. A few chronic addicts today set out to experiment with drugs and got stuck.

The National Institute on Drug Abuse shows that the same reasons for drug abuse exist in the United States. These reasons include the following:

- A desire to feel good (through feelings of pleasure, or a *high* feeling)

- A desire to feel better (for example, by relieving stress)

- A desire to do better (or improve performance)

- Curiosity and peer pressure

Research shows that the drug addiction rate among youths has reached alarming proportions. Years back, people were bothered by addiction to only one substance, but lately, they are bothered by addictions where people abuse many substances at the same time. Research done in 2016 shows that over six million bottles of codeine cough syrup have been sold in the north-west region of Nigeria, according to Umar Lawal Yusuf, Waziri Ahmed Gazali, and Musa Abdullahi.

Also, the National Drug Law Enforcement Agency report of 2010 shows that over 11 per cent of people in the same region abuse drugs. Substance abuse is now becoming very common among young people. Research has shown that about 40 per cent of Nigerian youths engage in substance abuse. A popular cliché says, "Youths are the leaders of tomorrow." But how could an addicted youth lead a country?

Commonly Abused Substances

Commonly abused substances come in different forms and preparations, and these are not limited to the following:

- **Tablets:** These include amphetamine (also known as ecstasy) and tramadol.

- **Sniffed substances:** These include glue, lizard and cow dung, human excreta, cocaine, matchstick head, petrol (PMS), cement, paint, and gutter water.

- **Smoked substances:** These include wrapped coffee, cigarettes, shisha (some flavoured), weed, marijuana (also known as *igboh*), and ganja.

- **Drinks:** These include cough syrup that contains codeine, *burukutu* (a fermented local alcoholic drink made from millet and guinea corn), monkey tail, *skoochies*, and other local alcoholic drinks viz *kaikai, ogogoro, akweteshi, pito,* and *Sapele water*).

- **Injectables:** These include pentazocine, anabolic steroids, and heroin.

Recently, substance abuse has taken another dimension in Africa, especially Nigeria. Teens and young adults have been implicated in the abuse of tramadol and cough syrup containing codeine. Many youths have overdosed on and died from tramadol abuse, while some chronically use cough syrup containing codeine. God placed a value on you by the blood of Jesus, bought you for a price, and brought you to be seated in heavenly places with Christ Jesus; don't choose the lowly place (1 Corinthians 7:23; Ephesians 2:6).

Effects of Substance Abuse

Substance abuse has grave effects. It may affect virtually all areas of life, including one's academics, personal life, parents, relationships, and country. Addiction may have the following effects.

Effects on Academics

- Addiction leads to truancy, low grades, or low performance.

- Addicts take longer to get through school.

- Addicts drop out of school.

Medical Effects

- Most abused substances are metabolized in the liver and may eventually damage the liver, resulting in chronic liver disease.

- Several studies have shown that some of those who abuse drugs also engage in unsafe sex and other risky behaviours, like sharing needles that promote the spread of HIV, hepatitis B and C, and other infectious blood-borne diseases.

- Drug addiction may lead to unwanted pregnancies in females.

- Inhaled substances can cause respiratory problems or even worsen existing or underlying ones, like asthma.

- When substances are abused over a long time, the immune system becomes weak, which also reduces the body's ability to fight disease.

- Drug addiction may cause a loss of appetite.

- Drug addiction may cause euphoria, dizziness, and mood changes.

- Drug addiction may cause a lack of ability to sustain activity.

- Drug addiction may impair thinking.

- Drug addiction may cause impotence.

- Drug addiction may cause a loss of one's sense of smell over time.

- Drug addiction may cause aggressiveness and irritability.

- Drug addiction may cause depression and other forms of mental illness.

- Drug addiction may lead to death.

Spiritual Effects

- Drug addiction may cause disconnection from God.

- Drug addiction may cause derailment in life and destiny.

- Drug addiction may lead to shame and reproach.

- Drug addiction may lead to eternal condemnation.

Physical Effects

- Drug addiction may make one prone to injuries, especially accidents.

- Drug addiction may lead to suicidal tendencies.

- Drug addiction may lead to homicide.

Familial Effects

- Drug addicts may tell serial lies to family members.

- Drug addicts may start stealing to get money so they can purchase the abused substances.

- Drug rehabilitation may place a huge financial burden on one's parents.

- Drug addiction may destabilize one's siblings and entire family.

- Drug addiction may disintegrate families and could send parents to early graves because of heartbreak.

National Effects

- Addiction drains a nation's economy.

- No addict can accomplish anything meaningful.

- No addict can effectively hold any important office of any country.

Very recently, it has been documented that some teen addicts infuse their drinks (fizzy drinks, local drinks, and so on) with abused substances, and some even add these substances to their meals, especially noodles, as "spice". A few teens have been drugged at parties because people tampered with their drinks or food and introduced substances to them. These cases have resulted in rape incidents.

Don't leave your drink, your food, or whatever you will consume unattended when you are not alone. Be careful where you go, who you associate with, and what you eat. (It is important to know that people who abuse substances usually try to mask this by using strongly scented perfumes and deodorants and even mouthwash or sweets.)

Addiction has no gain—only drain and endless pain. Depending on drugs, or constantly being high on any substance, makes you lose control of your life and destiny. If you lose control to substance abuse, it leads to self-destruction, an imminently slow suicide mission, and eternal condemnation.

Do you not know that when you continually offer yourself to someone (or to a substance) to do his will, you become the slave of the one you obey? You are a slave of either sin, which leads to death, or obedience, which leads to righteousness (Romans 6:16).

The Nigerian gospel group Freeborn has a song called "High" that has a very strong message:

> I'm on the high, am on the Most High; I don't need no tish to get me high.
>
> I understand am telling why am on the Holy Ghost am so high.........
>
> Why you dey take nicotine? I dey wonder.
>
> Why you believe alcohol is the answer?
>
> Why you allow heroin be your master?
>
> Why you dey talk, say nothing can ease your pain, and that's the reason why you take cocaine.
>
> Remember say Jesus is salvation for every situation.

Freeborn is a group of young people who stand for Christ; you, too, can stand for Christ.

God does not do drugs, but He's the Most High.

—Freeborn

Action Points

- No matter how "high" you have gotten on any substance, the Most High God would fix you. Repent and accept Jesus, and make a fresh start.

- You may need rehabilitation and the help of a behavioural scientist.

- Don't taste or try any drug or substance. Some teens who went that way are now addicts and have derailed their destiny.

> Jesus is the anchor for the soul.
>
> —John Hagee
>
> There's a sure way to get high! You can take a sip of the Spirit called *holy*.
>
> —Glowreeyah Braimah

Resources

- *Battlefield of the Mind for Teens* by Joyce Meyer

- American Psychiatric Association, 2018 https://www.psychiatry.org (help with addiction and substance use disorders)

- National Institute on Drug Abuse

- "High" by Freeborn

- "Drug Abuse among Youths in Nigeria: Implication to National Development" by Umar Lawal Yusuf, Waziri Ahmed Gazali, and Musa Abdullahi https://pdfs.semanticscholar.org

- Social media handle for Freeborn Nigeria Music group: Freebornng@iG; freebornNaija@Facebook; Freebornng@twitter

Chapter 12: Self-Image

Self-image is synonymous with self-regard, self-respect, and even self-perception. It also means how you think or how you see yourself based on your performance, your relationships, and even your appearance. It is good to know that self-image is merely your perception and may not reflect who you truly are. The truth about who you are is written in God's Word. His Word, the Bible, is the manual for self-perception and fully describes and documents your origin and identity.

As a child of God, how do you see yourself—as a winner or a loser? The head or the tail?

These are some self-image statements:

- "I am intelligent, and I know I can make it through to university."

- "I don't think I can make it to university."

- "I lose in most things, so I don't think the top is for me."

- "I would get to the top and be a trailblazer and a pacesetter."

Self-image can be either positive or negative, as the preceding declarations show. Your self-image is sometimes responsible for the inferiority or even superiority complex you experience or exhibit. Do you feel unaccepted or inferior because of your background? Your background has nothing to do with where God has ordained for you to be. A negative self-image leaves you with an inferiority complex that makes you think you are a loser.

Self-image is based on perception. So deliberately choose to see yourself as a success because, as Bishop David Oyedepo has said, "You cannot feature in a future you have not pictured." The people of Babel in the book of Genesis imagined building a tower to reach heaven. God knew that whatever humans pictured could come to pass because He gave man that capacity. He said "…God said let us go down, and there confound their language, that they may not understand one another's speech" (Genesis 11:7). You have the capacity to think *big* and become so. The devil is subtle; he will bring only ugly and inferior pictures

to you. Resist him, and he will flee! That is what the Bible says (James 4:7). Never let anyone scatter your psyche with negative words.

Your imagination is powerful. What do you imagine? When you look at yourself in the mirror, what do you see? Every child of God is a star! The potential to excel and become a phenomenon is built in you. You must perceive what God has designed you to be, and dare to utter it with boldness. Keep saying what you want to see with the requisite works, and it shall be so. Your self-image affects who you will become in life, and as far as you can see is what you can have. In the words of Sam Adeyemi, "You don't need to sleep to catch a dream; you only need your imagination to create the future you desire."

The Bible expressly states that God would do whatever you say into His ears (Numbers 14:28). Whatever you ask the Lord, He would do (John 16:23). A good self-image is built on self-worth that pivots on salvation.

Your self-worth should be high because you were purchased with the blood of Jesus. What monetary value could you possibly place on Jesus's blood? Jesus redeemed us into glory and honour, not reproach and shame.

Your self-worth will ultimately impinge upon your personality. Knowledge of who you are in Christ will catapult you into your predetermined destiny. When you have your self-image intact, your self-esteem and confidence will doubtlessly come alive, and you will soar. See you at the top!

The threefold ministry of the devil is to steal, kill, and destroy (John 10:10). When you allow the devil to steal your self-esteem, you experience the following:

- Frustration

- Lost glory and honour

- The experience of walking on foot, instead of riding horses

- Destiny derailment

Action Points

You can build a good self-image by doing the following:

- Renew your mind to have a positive self-image (Romans 12:1–2). Only God can give you that confidence to build your self-image.

- Hang around godly people who see the positive things in you.

- Know your Bible, know how God describes you in it, and hold on to it and not people's opinions.

- Write down *all* your dreams in a notebook and pronounce them daily because right words are forcible (Job 5:25). Boldly start doing those righteous and true things you have felt inferior about, and get on that roller coaster—thinking, voicing, and doing!

- Meditate on positive things.

- Draw up your strengths, and maximise them.

- Write down all your weaknesses, and improve on them with God's help.

- Have healthy Christian mentors in areas you seek to explore.

- Speak what you want to see. Create it with your mouth. Keep saying it until you see it.

- See yourself the way God sees you; to achieve that and have good success, you must meditate on God's Word day and night (Joshua 1:8).

You do not need anyone's special endorsement to fly. You are God's project, so the sky is your starting point.

Perception and reality are two different things.

—Tom Cruise

People see what they want to see, and what people want to see has nothing to do with the truth.

—Roberto Bolaño

Chapter 13: Loving the Body You Are In

You are beautifully and wonderfully made, and everything God made, He declared good (Genesis 1:31).

We all have unique looks and are built to fulfil our destiny, God's given purpose.

You know what? When God created the earth, He gave man dominion to rule over everything on earth (Genesis 1:28), but He gave no such authority to us to alter our build. He is the Potter, and we are the clay (Jeremiah 18:6). Before you were formed in your mother's womb, He knew you! Take note of this; He is the Former, not you! You are to maintain and take care of what He formed because we will all have to account for how we managed what He formed—that is, our bodies. He created your body as His temple (1 Corinthians 6:19), and if you destroy God's temple (1 Corinthians 3:17), you will have to account for that to God.

Recently, and frequently too, many of my teenage and even young adult friends have worried about their physiques and looks. What is happening? Some even seriously complain about the following:

- "I want to be taller."

- "I want to be light-skinned."

- "My boobs are too small."

- "My boobs are too big."

- "I am too fat. I really want to lose weight."

- "I feel so skinny. I want to put on some weight."

-

- "I wish I were a boy; boys' lives seem easier."

- "If I were a girl, I would have more attention and more money because I would be a slay queen."

We are in the last days, so take heed that you are not swayed by every form of doctrine (Ephesians 4:14). Whatever shape or size of body you find yourself in, give God the glory, love it, and nourish it.

Love Yourself

One of my teenage friends, Ike, revealed to me that his friends were all six-footers. Ike was the shortest among them, at five feet five inches. His friends were also muscle building to enlarge their biceps and develop the popular six-packs. This bothered Ike, as he was just thin; no matter what he did or ate, he saw no results. As a result, an inferiority complex, low self-esteem, and low self-worth had set in.

Do you find yourself in Ike's situation, or worse? Your looks and build are a combination of your parents' genetic makeup. You neither choose nor influence where you are born or which family you are born into. God brings you into the world through the *best* parents, your parents! Your looks are the best. Celebrate God, and thank Him for this. You are uniquely made.

You must see yourself the way God sees you and value yourself the way God does, and know that you are unique. If you don't value yourself, somebody else will value you wrongly. You don't need people's opinions to fulfil your destiny. All you need is in God's Word, so find out what God says concerning you because that is what matters. Take care of the body God has given you; love it, and nourish it. You are original, so do not distort the body God has created. Build a positive self-esteem, look at yourself in the mirror daily, and speak good things to you. "Speak consistently because ye shall have what ye say if ye doubt not" (Mark 11:23).

In the following flow chart, I have attempted to put down a sequence of events that may happen if you have a prolonged inferiority complex. Not everyone will follow the same

path; however, it is important to understand the chart and know that you are superior to everything low or inferior in your life.

Mind Your Company

The company you keep at this phase of life and beyond is extremely important. It can either mar you or make you. Your company defines the communications you have and ultimately determines your actions and inactions. The seeds of communication and action that you sow will germinate someday. Your company could influence you to love your body the way God made it or to act otherwise. You are unique and original; don't be someone's duplicate, except Christ's!

> You are a *masterpiece*.
>
> —Max Lucado
>
> Who you follow (virtually and otherwise) determines what follows you.
>
> —Bishop David Oyedepo

Use the following hashtags daily to put the devil where he belongs:

- #iambeautifullyandwonderfullymade

- #iamamasterpiece

- #iamunstoppable

- #icandoit

- #possibilitymentality

- #donotfaint

- #bebold!!

Chapter 14: Peer Pressure

Peer pressure means encouragement or influence by one's peer (British English Dictionary). Your peers could be your classmates and your friends who are your age. Peer pressure can be positive or negative. However, this term is most often used to connote bad influence. Peer pressure is the main battle or confrontation that teenagers face all through the teenage years and even into adulthood. It can span all phases of life.

As teenagers, peers tend to cling together, rub minds, experiment with things, and even venture into and undertake risky and dangerous tasks. They commonly take risks because they want to be like other peers who are their role models. In order for their peers not to label them *Jews* (inexperienced or naive) or *slackers* (dull or slow acting), they feel pressured to belong and fit in to cliques, groups, or cabals with tenets that may not necessarily sit well with the individuals. Moreover, every peer may indulge in a kind of vice, and if one is lured into such a group, clique, or cabal, it could derail, distort, or mar the person's destiny.

Some teenagers have also been positively influenced by peer pressure. They hung out with godly friends and, with God's help, made godly decisions in important areas of life, and are today's role models for upcoming teens.

Having interacted with a number of teenagers for a while now, I have realised a significant number of teens get into bad habits through friends because of negative peer pressure; they find themselves doing ungodly things. Initially, new entrants to these peer groups may engage in these new habits with some guilt and discomfort. Constantly engaging in these habits slowly deadens the conscience, and that means, without God's intervention, those teens are lost.

Peer pressure can affect what a teen wears, what a teen consumes, who a teen becomes friends with, how a teen styles his or her hair—the list can be endless. A few have also been pressured into having sex earlier than they should.

Negative peer pressure results in or manifests as the following:

- Having an early sexual debut or sexual perversions

- Consuming alcohol or binge-drinking

- Sneaking into night parties

- Breaking bounds

- Stealing to impress or belong

- Sniffing chemicals

- Taking illicit drugs and developing drug addictions

- Smoking (cigarettes, cocaine, weed, shisha, and so on)

- Cheating on examinations or plagiarising

- Developing social media addictions

- Forming unhealthy and unholy relationships

Positive peer pressure leads to the following acts:

- Living right by following biblical principles

- Fasting and praying as a lifestyle

- Shielding the self from every appearance of evil

- Maintaining healthy and holy relationships

In everything you want to do, pause and ask yourself, "Why am I doing this, and who do I want to please?" So what if you please the person? No human may see or even have a clue when you derail. But you know what? The Almighty, who cannot be deceived, sees every thought and action with His invisible CCTV camera. He is the one to fear—I mean reverently fear. He is all-knowing and all-seeing.

How do you spot negative peer pressure? Answer the following questions. If you respond yes to any of them, you face negative peer pressure.

- Do you feel guilty after you repeatedly do certain things?

- Do you feel depressed after such acts?

- Do you always try to please your friends and not make decisions of your own?

- Do you always seek your peers' approval for all you do?

- Do you always want to fit in and belong to the "happening guys"?

- Do you always want to be notorious for infamous acts?

- Do you damn your parents or guardians' counsel and lead your life your own way?

- Do you feel discomfort, guilt, or shame in sharing your experiences or acts with parents or guardians?

- Do you strongly desire the company of peers who you cannot introduce to your parents or tell your parents about?

- Do you have a stronger urge to indulge and conform to your peers' lifestyles (even though they're wrong) than to do the right thing?

- Are you living a double life with different personalities?

- Have you ever sworn an oath of secrecy—that is, keeping all secrets secret?

"Whatever you yield yourself to, you become a slave to it ... either of sin, which results in death, or of obedience, which results in being put right with God" (Romans 6:16).

The Bible explicitly records, "He will guard the feet of His godly ones, but the wicked shall be silenced and perish in darkness; for by strength shall no man prevail" (1 Samuel 2:9). This scripture clearly shows that God guards His own. Being under negative peer pressure and having involvement in any vices puts you under the wrath of God. Confess, forsake sin and cling to Jesus. A deep relationship with God guarantees the establishment of your glorious destiny and frees you from all negative pressure.

It is important to note that the enemy targets young people and families in subtle ways so he can destroy their lives and destinies, as seen in John 10:10: "The thief comes only to steal and kill and destroy."

But thank God for God, who has made for us all provisions to enjoy life through His son, Jesus Christ: "I came that they may have and enjoy life and have it in abundance" (John 10:10).

The following handle and reduce negative pressure:

- Stay closely knit with your family; share and discuss your dreams, fears, and challenges, and pray together.

- Start afresh with God through spiritual rehabilitation.

- Always speak the truth.

- Say no to ungodliness and worldly passion.

- Make your parents your friends, and learn to freely discuss things with them.

- Give your life to Christ, and be filled with the Holy Ghost.

Action Points

- Choose a godly life because living godly is a choice.

- Give your life to Christ so that He can empower you to live in a godly way.

- Let Jesus be the centre of all you do. Invite God daily into your life to help you handle your days and grant you the boldness to say no to *all* forms of ungodliness.

- Be a Word addict; read, meditate on, and study the Word of God.

- Remain committed to a Bible-believing church or fellowship.

- Develop your spiritual muscles through prayer and fasting.

Resources

- ReachOut.com (https://au.reachout.com)

> I'm not going to pretend I'm something I'm not so that you like me more.
>
> —Dan Pearce
>
> If you just set out to be liked, you would be prepared to compromise on anything at any time, and you would achieve nothing.
>
> —Margaret Thatcher
>
> Whatever you compromise to gain, you will lose.
>
> —Myles Munroe

Chapter 15: The Digitally Savvy Teen

Being a teenager is an exciting experience. Loads of adventure and exploration accompanies this phase of life. Teens are now living in a technology-laden world where they can access the globe on the spot with just a mobile phone. And social media places pressure on teens to learn more. In this process, some teens have crossed morally acceptable boundaries in a world of unlimited access, with solicited and unsolicited information that it may not be possible to handle rightly. Some teens have exposure to social media too early, and quite untimely exposure to some information too. This exposure has resulted in several kinds of habits and addictions that families, churches, and schools are battling with.

The benefits of social media are increasing by the day. Social media can promote:

- Instant communication and information sharing

- Digital marketing and advertising for services

- Evangelism

- Education and academics

These benefits may occur through Facebook, Pinterest, Instagram, Twitter, and Snapchat, just to mention a few. With the advent of these outlets, it has become imperative that teens know the benefits as well as the harmful effects of social media. Teens must have guidance on what to explore and how to surf the Internet.

Harmful effects of social media include the following:

- Many teens have developed very strong social media addictions, so their academics suffer; and these teens cannot fulfil their destinies.

- The secrets of individuals, friends, and even families have been brought to the public domain for discussion, which may sometimes attract harmful advice.

- Many vices have been spread and sometimes magnified on social media.

- Having virtual friendships with people you have never met before is risky, for some of these friends may be fake, and that has serious consequences. Many have gone so far as to accept marriage proposals on Facebook and other social media platforms when they are not ready for such intimate relationships.

- If you do not have discipline on social media platforms, you could waste a lot of time on things that only feed the flesh, and have no time to read the Bible and build your faith. When challenges come, you can't stand because your depth in God is shallow.

- People frequently post many ungodly and unsolicited posts on these platforms, and teens have no control over that. Exploring such can kill an enviable destiny. It takes only God to deliver a teen from pornography, nudity, and other sources of social media addiction.

Many addicted teens spend their time browsing and chatting away in the presence of God, even in church. This dishonours the Almighty God.

Action Points

- No matter how far gone your social media addiction is, retrace your steps, start afresh, and give your life to Jesus (Isaiah 1:18; John 3:16).

- Have a plan and stick to it (there is time for everything, so you should still have time for social media under parental guidance).

- Let your ways and actions honour God (Psalm 119:9, 16).

- Regularly engage in prayer and fasting while studying the Word.

- Be willing to talk about your challenges with parents.

Resources

- *"The Effects of Social Media on Mental Health"* by Megan Stonecipher

- *"What Are the Effects of Social Media on Youth?"* by Nick McGillivray

- Having virtual friendships with people you have never met before is risky, for some of these friends may be fake, and that has serious consequences. Many have gone so far as to accept marriage proposals on Facebook and other social media platforms when they are not ready for such intimate relationships.

- If you do not have discipline on social media platforms, you could waste a lot of time on things that only feed the flesh, and have no time to read the Bible and build your faith. When challenges come, you can't stand because your depth in God is shallow.

- People frequently post many ungodly and unsolicited posts on these platforms, and teens have no control over that. Exploring such can kill an enviable destiny. It takes only God to deliver a teen from pornography, nudity, and other sources of social media addiction.

Many addicted teens spend their time browsing and chatting away in the presence of God, even in church. This dishonours the Almighty God.

Action Points

- No matter how far gone your social media addiction is, retrace your steps, start afresh, and give your life to Jesus (Isaiah 1:18; John 3:16).

- Have a plan and stick to it (there is time for everything, so you should still have time for social media under parental guidance).

- Let your ways and actions honour God (Psalm 119:9, 16).

- Regularly engage in prayer and fasting while studying the Word.

- Be willing to talk about your challenges with parents.

Resources

- *"The Effects of Social Media on Mental Health"* by Megan Stonecipher

- *"What Are the Effects of Social Media on Youth?"* by Nick McGillivray

About the Author

Dr Uduak Essen is an international public health physician with an MBBS degree from the prestigious University of Nigeria, Nsukka. She is an alumnus of the London School of Hygiene and Tropical Medicine and the University of London and a fellow of the Royal Society for Public Health, all in the United Kingdom.

Her work has spanned the clinical and public health divisions of both the private and public sectors of the healthcare industry in Nigeria. She has coordinated and implemented several international research studies and surveys especially in HIV and other infectious diseases, as well as sickle cell disease.

She is a lover of God and has served with the children and evangelism units of the Living Faith Church at different times. Passionate about seeing children, especially teenagers, live for Christ, she has continuously guided teenagers and young adults as they navigate their path to adulthood. She had a burning unction to document most of her experience with teenagers and young adults in this manual, which she hopes will help more teens and young adults easily navigate their teenage years with God's help and become phenomena.

A multitalented public speaker, she is happily married with children.

Contact

Email: info@teenagerszone.com

Website: www.teenagerszone.com

Instagram: @teens.zone.unveiled

Twitter: @TZUnveiled

Printed in the United States
By Bookmasters